BLOOD and SILENCE

Kevin Farnham

Blood and Silence

Cover Art: Dale Farnham

ISBN: 978-0-9778833-4-9

Published by Everush Books

This book is available at EverushBooks.com and at online booksellers. The book may also be ordered through retail book stores using the ISBN number: 978-0-9778833-4-9.

*For you, my love,
my precious Dale!*

Prelude

The Circle

A cord around his leg, the hawk
Vainly tugs and rips and tears,
For he is down, can only walk.
Day after day he works; it wears.
The wings are stretched; Freedom is near.

He breathes the air, so glittering fresh.
It gives him flight. No thoughts make cold
His heart. He circles slowly, lives
Marked by crosslines in the scope.
A Shot! He's down, a claw in rope.

The Seaswan

That morning
I reflected sunglazed upon the dewdrop
Knowing it was true.

But sunrisinghigh
Sucked all away
Left me nakedparched clinging to
Diffused soulvapors irretrievable:
I burned in black light.

Now
I retire:
I will bathe in the sea and hope that
I, like the grimfaced
Seaswan who unheeding plunges
Overvulnerable whiteness into that
Graygrained saltwetness, will
Neither drown nor die for thirst.

Sunset on the Water Tower

Horizontal hair
whisking clouds
to distant ridges.

Cygnus

Emblem of sorrow, by the serpent pricked:
Double-eyed ever she flies.

Dante

He fired his world for world to see:
Beacon alone in bleak Italy.

Sea-Things

Cold restless shapes,
Armies on patrol,
They brush me

Or swallow me whole, and settle,
Amoeboid,
In the dark.

The Leaves Are Changing

the leaves are changing
color
      softly, slowly,
                          undiscernibly,
yet,
      tangibly:

      green
            into yellow
                      into orange
                        red
brown,
      into black

what splendor marks their flight
      into
      death

Bleeding Man

Nova

I burst upon the night-deep sky,
Streaming star where there was none;
Now my life is swallowed by
The dark and scatter of my blood.

The Bleeding Man

On this plain, grim desert fringe,
Burnt, cracked portal fronting Death,
Lies the bleeding man, alone,
A thousand miles from home.
Twenty years he fought the bloodless
Fiend, who parried his assaults
For sport, fending without shield;
He strode boldly, defiant,
Feeling with each inconsequent lunge
And swipe the power bleed from him.
Now he swoons, old man at last,
Frenzied heart jetting life from him,
Pumping all onto craving sands,
While bleached sun sears his parched cheek.

Hero's End

The fighting's done, the battle unwon,
But the severed heart beats on.

The Severed Heart

I am a severed heart,
Bleeding toward my death;
My body's ripped apart,
I've but this voice left.

A modern man I was,
Sucking science to my breast—
Till it became a monstrosity
And wracked my house to shreds.

I fought the bloodless fiend
With glittery sword and shield;
The battle was but dream,
Played out in fancy's field.

I chased him cross the plains
And watched him drown at sea;
Then he became the cliffs
That towered over me.

I chased the bloodied black fiend,
Lest others might his words attend;
But my weapons were mere fancies;
Against pure logic they could not defend.

Beware the fiend and all his deeds,
For I believed, and now am dead.
This voice is but my spirit's dream,
The words of the rose above my head.

The Unclasped Hand

Blood drips from the unclasped hand
Dribbling down the cold gray stair.

It's waiting there: the pickled flesh
Of a man who was your death.

Heartless Bleeding Man

Heartless bleeding man hears foaming waters,
waves beating, tolling incessant time. White
sea spray salts his open wounds, now parched.
And he is awake to pain and memory: a cav-
ern in his chest where once life was.

Strange spectacle: he sees it now, alive still,
but there, by itself, beyond his reach, alone:
his own heart excised, ripped out, flung away,
wasted on the sand, to die its own death while
he, numbed, watches. Frantically, ferociously,
it pumps away, jetting its dark deep life stream
onto vacant sands. Blood bubbles first, boils,
then is sucked down. But not without a trace:
grains dyed scarlet, stained with life, memory
retained.

He watches, oblivious to the cavity within
him, his own heart beating into death, frantic
thrusts now quieting, weakened toward somber
rest. And blustering winds blow rising sand
into his interior abyss, around the silenced heart,
burying all. His own memory fades as he watches,
life's blood exhausted, life work aborted, a life
complete yet undone.

Inward Sun

Alphabet

All Being Creates Day
Every Falling Gathers Hearing
In Joining Knowing Living Makes Name Of Prayer
Quiet Revealing Sighing The Union Void
World X Yes Zero

The is the Father.
Of is the Son.
In is the Holy Spirit.

KEVIN: Knowing Every Void In Name

He knows that words are little nothings
That divide the world into pieces.

In the Beginning

In name, the hearing earth begins every gathering. In name, name into name gathers. God of day created revealed Earth—all the Earth's days. The hearing Earth has ears all voicing every name's sign...

God's Name

God's name is I AM.
All that is is from Eternity.

Fragment from a Day
When Visions Were Seen

O sing me of the everush!
Tipping sing, Uinverse,
Every hush uttering!

... everings ...

heards
words of birds
burst

my head
a
heart:

HEAR "I AM"
EVER THESE WORDS
ARE THE ART

Universe

The Universe is meant to be a song:
one song.
One poem.
Uni-verse.

The World: it is each of us inverse:
our souls expressed
into material being:
u-in-verse: You-in-verse.
A song made of our lives.

Earth

Earth means Ear:
we are listeners, all of us.
Listeners to the light,
to the words life
whispers in our hearts.

Earth means Hearing.
Earth means Hearth.

Earth means Art:
our lives are our Art.
They are our Creation.

God gives us to create the universe.
It is what we make it.

God makes us.
We decide who we will be.
Our decision makes the Universe.

Ruined "I"

In the dark wood of my soul,
I came upon myself:
a letter "I" made of stone,
in ruins:

prostrate,
cracked,
brittle,
wind-pocked,
weatherbeaten.

Vegetation growing around the base,
eyeless worms squirming beneath
the wet, mudded, supine form,
bugs crawling on the top and sides,
acid lichens dissolving its exposed surface.

Cracked and worn such that
it could never stand again.
Were any to try to raise it, stand it up,
it would fracture irrevocably,
collapse and crumble into
dry stony pieces
and dust.

Radiant Star

Radiant star,
You are my sight,
Endless streaming
In the night;

And I'm a glass
That but refracts
The life you are,
The world you make.

Silence Is Your Name

Silence is your name,
Silence the name you gave me;
But bless this broken totem
(Round which ragged worlds have gathered),
For I am a fallen man,
My 'I' a fallen world.

O sweet silent wonder,
Let words gather and be still
As hushed they once whirled in awe
Round their living sun, and breathe
Into me your whispering dew;
Make me, dear Lord, anew!

Within and Without

There is no without that has not been within.
All that is before us has been forged within,
and mirrors that within in all its complexity.
What I experience in the world, what I see
and hear and smell and taste and touch, is the
ever changing image of all that is behind me,
that is, history.

History? His story. Who's story? Man's
story. The phenomena of the world are im-
ages forged since the beginning of time in the
souls of men. Look: that hawk who circles
stoically above the desolate bare-treed hill: how
is it that he has arrived there? Just so have
similar hawks circled before the eyes of men
for millenia upon millenia. But not quite so,
for their hearts were different. This particu-
lar hawk you and I see today is but the son of
those thousand others, and not identical with
them. For they were the phenomena of our
fathers' worlds, and circled hilltops made in
the image of our fathers' hearts, their within,
which included our own but in potentia.

But how did there come to be any hawk-
like thing? What of that first hawk, from whom
all others descended, the hawk that Adam first

saw? Surely it leaped from his heart into the phenomenal world the moment he felt it stir and gave it its name! Originally the Word had implanted it there, and hawk and heart had been one, and nameless. Who knows how long it had circled those desolate reaches within his soul and beyond his vision, crying out to him, before finally he took notice? But in naming it he set it free: what had existed but in potential suddenly became reality, an actual phenomenal entity that could be seen and heard and remembered, all because of the word. Man had set the hawk and his heart apart, with but the word in between, and indeed his heart then was hawkless, and hollowed. The Word had been fractured and a manword made: a space between two that had been one. And time had begun.

What I see before me is an ever changing image, image of the life of man. For space and time are born of words: the expanse of space is but an expanse of words, a perceptual projection composed in language, in emptiness, and all distance is but the disjunction between man and his phenomena, which once were one in the Word.

Look at the world, and look at man. See

the outer edge, but too the inner. The outer edge we "see" only with the aid of radio telescopes, instrumentation—that is, in theory. We "see" the edge of the universe, the edge of matter, and it recedes from us at the speed of light. What is it that we find there? Nothing but the rattlings of that bang which marks, in theory, that innermost edge of the within—namely, the Beginning. In the outermost, most unreachable edge of space is found the image of the nethermost, most unknowable edge of time. Is it any surprise?

In man lies all history: the past, which recedes within him as he lives his paltry Earth life, an inward movement reflected in the outward expansion at the speed of light of his phenomenal world, whose edge appears equidistant from him regardless of where he chooses to fix his gaze, that distance equal to the distance a ray of light would travel in the time from the theoretical beginning of the universe to the present—equidistant, as though the "Big Bang" had occurred right here, on Earth, in the hearts of men, so many billions of ago, when Adam spoke that first, fatal word.

There is no without that has not been within. And there is no within that lacks potential to become an imaged without. Man occupies the centerpoint, and all nature is formed in his image. That's his story.

Awareness and Namelessness

Only that which proceeds from awareness and returns by nature to namelessness is possible; all else is illusion.

The Waters

Body

The body is a garden infused with a sliver of awareness.

Death and Life

Only death addicts us; life is freedom.
Only life can melt away death.
Only what is real can scatter what is unreal.

Emptiness 1

What is emptiness
but a spot in the universe
where life should have been—but isn't?

Emptiness 2

We cannot give by creating emptiness in ourselves. All we can do is cover up a valley of sorrow—but at the cost of creating an emptiness that is greater than what would have been suffered had we simply lived the highest possible love we could, and given that love in the moment of need, and forever.

We cannot smooth over valleys of sorrow without creating a greater sorrow and uncertainty that shadows our entire life, because love that would have been had the sorrow been traversed is not—and the lack is felt: an emptiness that seems to have come from nowhere—yet is truly felt.

If we turn away from the sorrow, by turning away from the love—surely we also turn away from the joy—and leave a life that is flat—level, but unfulfilled.

Please—love everything that you know is true. Please don't turn away and say "It's impossible." There is only one love. And that love has no limits, except for those we erect ourselves, as roadblocks in our lives and the lives of everyone we love—beyond which no love may penetrate—and within which all emptiness arises.

Emptiness 3

And emptiness is the only enemy we face in this world. And an undefeatable enemy at that—because it is nothing but absence of what should be there, filling the universe: life.

Emptiness has no being, so how do you fight it? Every time you reach out to touch it, you die, and the part of you that touched it is no longer there, living as a part of your being.

It's suicide ever to willingly reach out for it, that's all.

Sacrifice

And even love is confused and disoriented when Life commands that love be sacrificed, even for love. Because love does not understand the division of this world, and how love can possibly seem to be at odds with love—and how even though love itself is one, the spaces between people can be unbridgeable—and how people can suffer in weakness of will to love, and die rather than love.

The world is stupid, materialistic, and idolatrous. Our hearts know what change has taken place, and what it means.

Sacrifice.

The river had flowed in a certain direction, and now meets there an obstacle, unpenetrable, unmeltable. And it swirls around the obstacle, a great dark boulder in the riverbed—and the waters are confused. For the waters, at their creation, at the beginning of time, had been given a desire, and a strength, to fill that spot in the riverbed, with love and hope and life. Yet the world has made at that point an unpenetrable obstacle.

And so, the waters turn away—but not without confusion, and lack of understanding. The love that would have been: how can it understand?

Find a new home for it. Call it. Ask it to come, to stop swirling about the boulder it cannot penetrate. Tell it to come with the river itself, and not cry over what could not be. Tell it to come and sing with us, and love the love we give one another. Ask it not to tarry, and endlessly swirl and touch the edges of darkness it cannot bring to life.

Taboo

There are some questions for which the least untruthful answer is silence. Denial is a lie. Yet, to summon an image of darkness that wanders only the void of the past (because it has been put to death) into a fully lit living and growing present, is to counterfeit that present (by creating new darkness where light is meant to be)—hence, to sin.

Once lost, light can never be recovered fully. A speck endures, shriven calcification of soul, spacetime singularity speaking in silence: "Someone died here." Graven inlet, it always will be findable if one searches, even amid utterly reformed born-again existence. And if one looks deeply into it, as into a backward-pointing lens, probes with it, beckons, stirring quieted pools of nothingness, voided darkness can be witnessed, made visible, and, should faith falter (which it mustn't), wakened.

Our lives, indeed, are fragile. All love is. This moment only is real. What would we have reality be? Surely the only life-sustaining possibility is to blind our eyes to all darkness, past and potential, to let the present well into being and fill all existence with its new light,

light that has never before been seen or expe-
rienced.

And apologize for instantiation of taboo,
this void of silence.

Eden Morning

Eden

You asked me once about Eden—what I thought about it—if it was a real place, where it is—

When that light pours in across our sky, creating the heavens before our eyes, with light that shines outward from within us—there we begin to live in Eden. Because that light, I believe, is the light that shines from Eden into this curtained world. And when we come to that place, and drop all complications of our earthly personality, and live in one loving essence— then, that light, that beautifully beating, breathing, ushing light raises us into Eden by wrapping us in the images, the world, the life that simply is, forever, Eden.

Love

Love is a river of light,
born within us,
from beyond the center of our being.

It flows through us,
asking us to live its life,
to make this earth in its image.

Before

Before I knew my love,
I knew a world that was dying, and
a heaven that was striving to be
but somehow couldn't find
its way into existence.

I knew what had to be, because
life has granted me vision.
But instead of making the world
become what I knew it was in truth,
my actions parted with
the light of my visions,
and I created for my home an
expansive universe pocked with
deathly emptiness.

I saw light coming in at the center, but
instead of living this truth into the world,
I often created Hell.
My mind was betraying my soul, and
the life I knew should have been
was becoming an aching death.

The Monks

Those who live alone do not know
the meaning of love on this earth.

The monks know God.
They find love
in the center of their souls,
shining out over them,
like an inward sun.
They feel the warmth of this sun.
Its love beckons them.
The monk who follows his light
finds truth, finds life.

But the life he finds is not that
of this earth, but of eternity in itself,
the paradise that has never fallen.
That is where he seeks to live.
That world is his goal.

But God did not create
this earth and humankind
solely that they would learn
to reject a corrupt world and
turn within to find Him.
He created this earth
to be paradise.

That same paradise
which the monks find within
is meant to live on earth as well.
The monks are not wrong to turn
to God within themselves:
for it is solely from within
that they are called.

Fear 1

There are those who have not found
the one they need,
but fear to leave the one they are with
out of fear of loneliness.

This is a trap that can only lead to greater
unhappiness than the loneliness itself.
One who fears loneliness
lacks the courage to be all that his soul
asks him to be.

One does not live in this world
without courage.
Truth cannot be lived
if one shuns difficulties.

Fear 2

Fear has no place in this world.
Life cannot be guided by fear.
Only death is guided by fear.

To live, to love, we must live
by our best, most faithful estimate
of where the path to truth lies.

Admittedly, it is our imperfect
judgment that we must live by.
Yet, living by judgment leads to
perfection.

Those who are ruled by fear always find
a world far worse than their worst fears.

Those who seek to avoid a suffering
that lies along the path of truth,
the path to life,
inevitably end up creating
for themselves and those who love them
a worse suffering
than that which they feared
and away from which they turned.

Deception

To accept an imperfect life
is to turn away from the path
leading to perfection and fulfillment.

To turn away from the path
that leads to true life
is to turn onto a road that
leads to darkness and sorrow and despair.

How can you give to someone
you know is not the one you need?
If you pretend to her that she is that one,
you have lied to her and not given
your entire self.

Thus, you cheat her of your true love,
and give her something that cannot possibly
help her to find the life her soul
has promised her.

If the deception is sufficiently flawless,
you guide her into a hell you create
for both her and yourself.

You have betrayed her too,
not just yourself.
You have made her also the victim of your
inadequacy.

And in the end, you realize that
it would have been far better
to have been honest from the start,
both with her and with yourself.

We lie to each other.
We lie to ourselves.

Shadowland

We cannot be what we are
unless we have our center.
Lovers cannot be who they are meant to be
unless they first find their beloved.

She is the key.
He is the key.

Either all doors will be unlocked,
or all will remain closed.

Either a lover will faithfully persevere,
searching every last corner of the universe
until he finds the one he needs,
or despair will defeat love's purpose,
and an entire life will be spent
in a shadowland.

Indeed, many in the shadowland are deemed
wonderful successes by the world.
They put what energy they have into
worldly labors,
because they have given up all of their
heart's and soul's desires.

But these people are not
what they could have been.
They do not change the world for the better.
They live on the talents of their
minds and bodies.

But these are nothing
compared to the genius
that would have been
had mind and body been united
with heart and soul,
all inspired by the light of
eternal fulfillment.

The Grandest Illusion

I wrote these words:

> *I burst upon the night-deep sky,*
> *Streaming star where there was none;*
> *Now my life is swallowed by*
> *The dark and scatter of my blood.*

A nova is born in a
spectacular blaze of light.
But it quickly collapses,
fades into a dim
white dwarf star,
engulfed by an ever-expanding shell
of dark star matter
that gives off
no light
of its own.

This was my blood:
the light that should have been,
but somehow had failed to come to be.

All those who give up
the search for the beloved end
in this condition.
They are meant to love on this earth,
but have given in to despair
and now lack faith,
doubting even that their beloved exists.
They cannot find anything in themselves,
even if they have been granted
a clear vision of what is meant to be,
because they have given up hope.
They have decided the universe is not perfect,
after all,
that all their visions
of love and joy were illusions.

Yet this belief itself
is the grandest illusion
of all. It is the one lie
that makes all lies believable.

Suffering

A suffering which lies in
the path leading to life
is lit by the love that
draws the traveler
toward his end.

And though he may not see this light
at the time, in being the light of truth,
it is sufficient to sustain him in his trial.

But a suffering created by fear of life
contains no sustaining light,
because the suffering is shrouded
in its victim's fear and cowardice,
which created it.

It is not part of the path to life,
and so contains no sustenance,
unless through it the sufferer discovers
the error of his bowing to fear,
and so turns away from fear.

Earthly Love

Earthly love is a circle of light.
The light travels both ways
around the circle,
so that every creation is lighted
both from within and without.

The sun shines within me,
just as it does for the monks.
But, for me, another sun shines,
lighting me from the outside too.
The sun within my love shines through her life
and into me.
And the light from her touches me
and warms me,
and I become everything the light within me
has always told me I must be.

Loving

I search for my love's center,
to love her there,
with the deepest love in me,
with the peak of my being,
so that she will know everywhere who I am
and what my love is.

I search
for the place in her where
all life flows into her, where
she ceases to recognize her own being
because everything she sees is
love and light.

And that love flows into her
of its own accord.
And her first recognition is that
it is love for me,
born from a place beyond her, yet
flowing into her deeply, boundlessly,
and becoming her own.

It is me
loving her from beyond herself
that she feels—
me loving her from paradise,
where we were born,
where our souls shall always live,
with the love life has given us
to give to one another,
forever.

The Path

My love and I walk
along a path by the river.
The shore is lit by the light of the waters,
but still we sometimes stumble and fall.
We are not perfect.

This is a path leading to paradise.
But only the perfect feel paradise
in every moment.
We know it is there in every moment, and
we know we are getting nearer to the peak
of this mountain,
nearer to the river's source.
But some moments we are lost,
and we rely on love and faith
until we find the path again.

I Face My Love

I face my love,
and she is my light, my world.
In her is the fulfillment of my every need
and desire.

In giving her all, I have all.
In finding all for her, I gain all
that my heart and soul and mind and body
have ever needed to find.

I face my love,
and I am face to face with my life.

I Love You Dale

I dreamed of you so long ago:

Love ushing in the Eden morning,
Oceans welling, eternally born,
Voices singing all creatures to life.
Eden, indeed—but for me, a dream.

You lighted within me, butterfly!
Out of heart's deep night you have come,
Uttering life with your every word.

Dale! You are my soul afire!
All creation shines in you—
Lighting the way to all my dreams,
Eden welling: my love in you.

The Gateway

Toward a gateway framed in petals
you draw me—
I, who have walked a dust-ridden path,
and spent many nights lying on stones—
your sacred emblem beckons me.

I enter the castle:
warmth and life and song.
Your voice soothes me, caresses,
entices me to life.

You touch me deeply, and I am home.
I begin to see you where you live:
in perfect loving giving.
Softly you call me still.
I begin to see...

Song sparrows stir,
then dash across the sky.
The galaxies awakened sing.
Borne in a rushing ribbon of light
we melt in sparkles across the night,
and silent dew drops radiant on our life.

www.ingramcontent.com/pod-product-compliance
Lightning Source LLC
Chambersburg PA
CBHW021144020426
42331CB00005B/894

* 9 7 8 0 9 7 7 8 8 3 3 4 9 *